# When You Reach Me

Rebecca Stead

## STUDENT PACKET

**NOTE:**

The trade book edition of the novel used to prepare this guide is found in the Novel Units catalog and on the Novel Units website. Using other editions may have varied page references.

Please note: We have assigned Interest Levels based on our knowledge of the themes and ideas of the books included in the Novel Units sets, however, please assess the appropriateness of this novel or trade book for the age level and maturity of your students prior to reading with them. You know your students best!

---

BN 978-1-60878-125-6

opyright infringement is a violation of Federal Law.

2020 by Novel Units, Inc., St. Louis, MO. All rights reserved. No part of s publication may be reproduced, translated, stored in a retrieval system, or nsmitted in any way or by any means (electronic, mechanical, photocopying, cording, or otherwise) without prior written permission from Novel Units, Inc.

production of any part of this publication for an entire school or for a school stem, by for-profit institutions and tutoring centers, or for commercial sale is ictly prohibited.

ovel Units is a registered trademark of Conn Education.

inted in the United States of America.

To order, contact your
local school supply store, or:

Toll-Free Fax: 877.716.7272
Phone: 888.650.4224
3901 Union Blvd., Suite 155
St. Louis, MO 63115

sales@novelunits.com

novelunits.com

# Note to the Teacher

Selected activities, quizzes, and test questions in this Novel Units® Student Packet are labeled with the following reading/language arts skills for quick reference. These skills can be found above quiz/test questions or sections and in the activity headings.

**Basic Understanding:** The student will demonstrate a basic understanding of written texts. The student will:
- use a text's structure or other sources to locate and recall information (Locate Information)
- determine main idea and identify relevant facts and details (Main Idea and Details)
- use prior knowledge and experience to comprehend and bring meaning to a text (Prior Knowledge)
- summarize major ideas in a text (Summarize Major Ideas)

**Literary Elements:** The student will apply knowledge of literary elements to understand written texts. The student will:
- analyze characters from a story (Character Analysis)
- analyze conflict and problem resolution (Conflict/Resolution)
- recognize and interpret literary devices (flashback, foreshadowing, symbolism, simile, metaphor, etc.) (Literary Devices)
- consider characters' points of view (Point of View)
- recognize and analyze a story's setting (Setting)
- understand and explain themes in a text (Theme)

**Analyze Written Texts:** The student will use a variety of strategies to analyze written texts. The student will:
- identify the author's purpose (Author's Purpose)
- identify cause and effect relationships in a text (Cause/Effect)
- identify characteristics representative of a given genre (Genre)
- interpret information given in a text (Interpret Text)
- make and verify predictions with information from a text (Predictions)
- sequence events in chronological order (Sequencing)
- identify and use multiple text formats (Text Format)
- follow written directions and write directions for others to follow (Follow/Write Directions)

**Critical Thinking:** The student will apply critical-thinking skills to analyze written texts. The student will:
- write and complete analogies (Analogies)
- find similarities and differences throughout a text (Compare/Contrast)
- draw conclusions from information given (Drawing Conclusions)
- make and explain inferences (Inferences)
- respond to texts by making connections and observations (Making Connections)
- recognize and identify the mood of a text (Mood)
- recognize an author's style and how it affects a text (Style)
- support responses by referring to relevant aspects of a text (Support Responses)
- recognize and identify the author's tone (Tone)
- write to entertain, such as through humorous poetry or short stories (Write to Entertain)
- write to express ideas (Write to Express)
- write to inform (Write to Inform)
- write to persuade (Write to Persuade)
- demonstrate understanding by creating visual images based on text descriptions (Visualizing)
- practice math skills as they relate to a text (Math Skills)

Name _____

*When You Reach Me*
Activity #1 • Prereading
Use Before and After Reading
*(Prior Knowledge/Making Connections)*

## Anticipation and Reaction

**Directions:** Consider the following statements before you read the novel. Place a checkmark in one of the boxes to show whether you agree or disagree with each statement, and provide your reasoning. After you have completed the novel, mark your response again. Provide an explanation if your opinion has changed.

| Statement | Response Before Reading | Response After Reading |
|---|---|---|
| "It's crazy the things a person can pretend not to notice" (p. 18). | ☐ you agree with the statement<br>☐ you disagree with the statement | ☐ you agree with the statement<br>☐ you disagree with the statement |
| | | |
| "A person can't miss something [s/he] never had" (p. 28). | ☐ you agree with the statement<br>☐ you disagree with the statement | ☐ you agree with the statement<br>☐ you disagree with the statement |
| | | |
| "Sometimes you never feel meaner than the moment you stop being mean" (p. 144). | ☐ you agree with the statement<br>☐ you disagree with the statement | ☐ you agree with the statement<br>☐ you disagree with the statement |
| | | |
| "…the secret of traveling through time…is a thing so incredible that most people would consider it a miracle" (p. 193). | ☐ you agree with the statement<br>☐ you disagree with the statement | ☐ you agree with the statement<br>☐ you disagree with the statement |
| | | |

Name _____

**When You Reach Me**
Activity #2 • Prereading
Use Before Reading
*(Predictions)*

## Computer Blog

**Directions:** Listed below are some of the chapter titles from the novel. Beside each title, predict one or two "things" you think could be important in the chapter. Then, on the lines below, predict what you think will happen in the novel.

| Chapter Titles | Your Predictions |
|---|---|
| Things That Get Tangled | |
| Things You Keep Secret | |
| Things You Don't Forget | |
| Things You Push Away | |
| Things That Make No Sense | |
| Things That Turn Upside Down | |
| Things That Heal | |
| Things You Protect | |

_____
_____
_____
_____
_____
_____

Name _____

*When You Reach Me*
Activity #3 • Vocabulary
Things You Keep in a Box–
Mom's Rules for Life in New York City

## Vocabulary Multiple Choice

| obstruct | omen | budget | fundamental |
| burden | scoured | expired | prosecutor |
| attorney | swivel | tenant | processed |
| radiators | theories | obvious | |

**Directions:** Choose the BEST definition for each vocabulary word as it is used in the novel.

____ 1. obstruct
 (a) block
 (b) blotch
 (c) magnify

____ 2. omen
 (a) ritual
 (b) sign
 (c) truth

____ 3. budget
 (a) funds
 (b) math
 (c) value

____ 4. fundamental
 (a) basic
 (b) random
 (c) special

____ 5. burden
 (a) disaster
 (b) freight
 (c) responsibility

____ 6. scoured
 (a) contaminated
 (b) polished
 (c) searched

____ 7. expired
 (a) divided
 (b) infected
 (c) outdated

____ 8. prosecutor
 (a) juror
 (b) prisoner
 (c) public officer

____ 9. attorney
 (a) criminal
 (b) lawyer
 (c) reporter

____ 10. swivel
 (a) bend
 (b) coil
 (c) rotate

____ 11. tenant
 (a) owner
 (b) renter
 (c) ruler

____ 12. processed
 (a) paraded
 (b) prepared
 (c) sold

____ 13. radiators
 (a) detectors
 (b) heaters
 (c) valves

____ 14. theories
 (a) facts
 (b) illusions
 (c) opinions

____ 15. obvious
 (a) apparent
 (b) cautious
 (c) sly

Name _____

***When You Reach Me***
Activity #4 • Vocabulary
Things You Wish For–
Things You Keep Secret

## Vocabulary Chart

| nonexistent | official | panic | linoleum |
| hexagonal | et cetera | prolong | warped |
| reveal | technology | proposal | pathetic |
| revolved | assumption | physics | |

**Directions:** Write each vocabulary word in the left-hand column of the chart. Complete the chart by placing a checkmark in the column that best describes your familiarity with each word. Working with a partner, find and read the line where each word appears in the story. Find the meaning of each word in the dictionary. Together with your partner, choose six of the words checked in the last column. On a separate sheet of paper, use each of those words in a sentence.

| Vocabulary Word | I Can Define | I Have Seen/Heard | New Word For Me |
|---|---|---|---|
| | | | |
| | | | |
| | | | |
| | | | |
| | | | |
| | | | |
| | | | |
| | | | |
| | | | |
| | | | |
| | | | |
| | | | |
| | | | |
| | | | |

Name _____

***When You Reach Me***
Activity #5 • Vocabulary
Things That Smell–Messy Things

## Vocabulary Comprehension

| despise | blaring | disaster | reaction |
| distracted | postscript | veil | cruelty |
| preservatives | offense | irritating | |

**Directions:** Circle the answer that shows the meaning of each vocabulary word as it is used in the novel.

1. If you despise sports, do you love or hate baseball?

2. If an alarm is blaring, is the sound harsh or gentle?

3. The recital is a disaster. Is the event a success or a failure?

4. Your mother expects a reaction. Does she want a response or silence?

5. If you are distracted, are you focused or sidetracked?

6. A letter has a postscript. Is it at the beginning or end?

7. If someone peers through a veil, is the view hazy or clear?

8. Does cruelty demonstrate meanness or kindness?

9. Is food containing preservatives more likely to cook faster or last longer?

10. If your friend takes offense, is she insulted or honored?

11. A rash is irritating. Is it soothing or annoying?

**When You Reach Me**
Activity #6 • Vocabulary
Invisible Things–
Things That Make No Sense

Name _____

## Vocabulary Scramble and Definitions

| mimeographs | circulation | jailbird | epilepsy |
| precious | seizures | construct | teleportation |
| atoms | triumphant | mystified | insane |
| justification | | | |

**Directions:** Unscramble the vocabulary words using the definitions as clues.

1. _____ upsorcei — valued; beloved

2. _____ blajirid — prisoner

3. _____ pahnttmuir — rejoicing over success; victorious

4. _____ sirezuse — attacks; convulsions

5. _____ nesain — senseless; without reason

6. _____ peltainrootte — instantly moving from one place to another

7. _____ geomirshmap — copies created by a printing machine that uses inked stencils

8. _____ desmitify — bewildered; confused

9. _____ scorncutt — a complex idea or theory

10. _____ luccainoirt — valid use as currency

11. _____ ascifitujoint — good reason; explanation that defends an action

12. _____ motas — smallest portion of an element; basic units of matter

13. _____ seeppily — disorder of the nervous system

Name _____

**When You Reach Me**
Activity #7 • Vocabulary
The First Proof–
The Second Proof

## Synonyms/Antonyms

| swaggered | hypnotizing | hysterical | dissolved |
| sesame | miserable | vision | appropriate |
| remotely | valuable | symbolize | sincere |
| racist | dingy | microscopic | |

**Directions:** Each of the words below is either a synonym or an antonym of a vocabulary word. Write the related vocabulary word on the line. Circle the words that are synonyms, and underline those that are antonyms.

1. solidified _____

2. image _____

3. prejudiced _____

4. spellbinding _____

5. worthless _____

6. dull _____

7. seed _____

8. unfitting _____

9. genuine _____

10. shuffled _____

11. happy _____

12. slightly _____

13. gigantic _____

14. represent _____

15. uncontrollable _____

Name _____

***When You Reach Me***
Activity #8 • Vocabulary
Things in an Elevator–
Things That Heal

## Vocabulary Concentration

| deliberately | frantic | decade | sheer |
| non-judgmental | sacrifice | determination | meditating |
| supervise | torment | heap | miracle |
| observation | raving | conspiracy | |

**Directions:** To create game cards, work with a partner to make two sets of cards using the vocabulary words above. On the first set, write each vocabulary word (one word per card). On the second set, write each vocabulary word's definition (one definition per card). Only write on one side of the card. (See the sample cards below.)

**Game Instructions:** Shuffle both sets of cards together. Spread the cards facedown on a table. Player One turns over two cards. If the player matches a vocabulary word with its definition, the player keeps both cards and takes another turn. If the cards do not match, Player One returns them to their places on the table. Then Player Two takes a turn. Continue playing until all cards have been matched correctly. The player with the most cards wins.

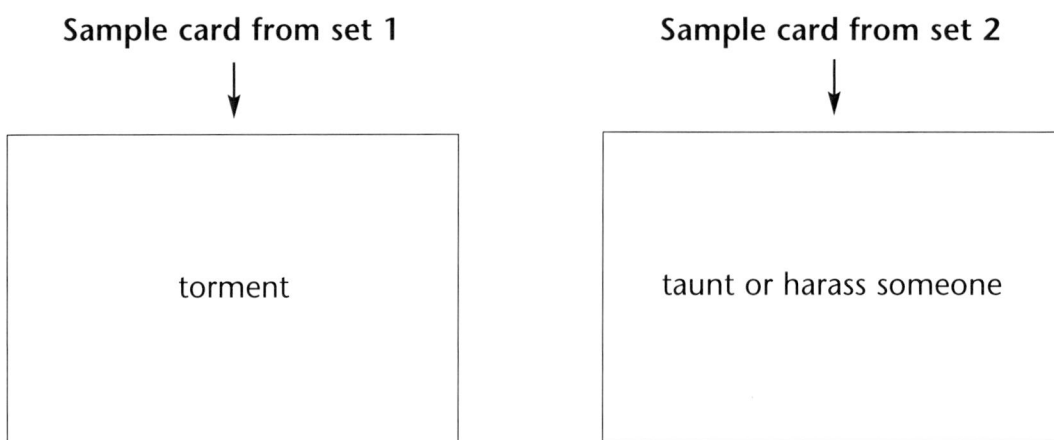

Sample card from set 1: torment

Sample card from set 2: taunt or harass someone

Name _____

*When You Reach Me*
Activity #9 • Vocabulary
Things You Protect–
Parting Gifts

## Word Map

| casually | sprinted | accusingly | anesthesia |
| allegations | embroidered | audience | podium |
| artificial | autographs | squawked | precise |
| applications | seam | | |

**Directions:** Choose seven vocabulary words from the list above. Examine how each word is used in the novel, and then complete a word map for each word.

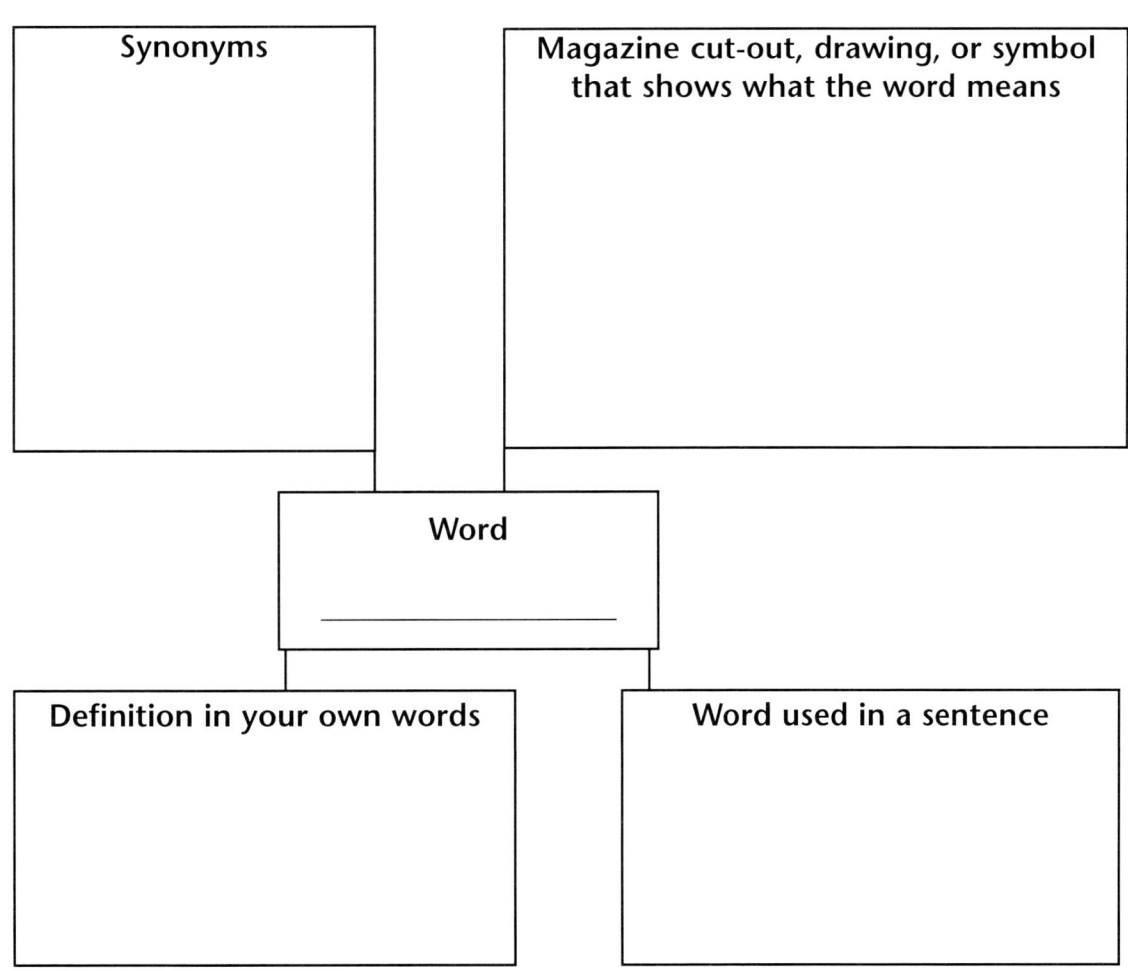

© Novel Units, Inc. 11

Name _____

**When You Reach Me**
Study Guide

**Directions:** Answer the following questions on a separate sheet of paper. Starred questions indicate thought or opinion questions. Use your answers in class discussions, for writing assignments, and to review for tests.

## Things You Keep in a Box–Mom's Rules for Life in New York City

1. Where is Mom going on April 27, 1979?
2. What does Miranda keep in a box under her bed? Who gave these items to her?
3. Why does Mom call Richard "Mr. Perfect"? How does Richard react?
*4. Why does Mom steal supplies from the office? Do you think the reason justifies her actions?
5. What is the first line of Miranda's favorite novel?
6. When did Mom quit law school?
7. Where do Mom and Miranda hide the spare apartment key?
8. Why did Miranda think of herself and Sal as being inseparable?
9. What does the laughing man mumble under his breath?
10. What do Richard and Miranda do when trying to solve a problem?
11. What begins on the day Sal gets punched? What ends?
12. What is Miranda's trick for dealing with people who frighten her?

## Things You Wish For–Things You Keep Secret

1. For what does Miranda blame her dad?
2. Why does Miranda refer to the wish list on the fridge as the "official list"?
3. Why does talking to the kid in the green jacket make Miranda feel guilty?
*4. Why do you think Sal no longer wants to be friends with Miranda?
5. How is Julia different from the other students?
6. Why does Miranda ask Annemarie out to lunch?
*7. What does Annemarie's room tell you about her?
8. What does Miranda mean by "big money"?
9. What project is Miranda's class building?
10. Who is Wheelie? What job does she give Miranda?
11. How does Marcus behave oddly around Miranda?
12. Why does Marcus tell Miranda she is "a pretty smart kid" (p. 52)?

Name _____

***When You Reach Me***
Study Guide
page 2

## Things That Smell–Messy Things

1. What does Colin ask Jimmy?
2. Why does Miranda run down to Sal's apartment?
3. What makes Mom certain that she did not forget to lock the door?
4. Where does Miranda find the first note?
5. Why can't Miranda help customers as Annemarie and Colin do?
6. What does the laughing man call Annemarie?
7. Where does Miranda find the second note?
8. What is in Jimmy's Fred Flintstone bank?
9. According to Mom, what happens when someone lifts his or her "veil"?
10. What is Miranda's nickname for Julia?
*11. Why does Miranda feel strange when she looks at Colin?
*12. Do you think Miranda is starting to act like the other girls? Why or why not?

## Invisible Things–Things That Make No Sense

1. Why is Miranda invisible to Marcus?
2. What does Jimmy tell Julia to do?
3. What does Mom do once every month?
4. What did the robber take?
5. Why do the students have to eat lunch in the school cafeteria?
* 6. What happens to Annemarie at lunch? How do you think the school nurse knew?
7. Why does Annemarie's dad have her on a special diet?
*8. Whom does Miranda think left a rose for Annemarie? Whom do you think left the rose?
9. Where does Miranda find the third note?
10. What does "tesser" mean?
11. What does Julia use to explain time travel?
12. Why did Marcus hit Sal?

Name _____

**When You Reach Me**
Study Guide
page 3

## The First Proof–The Second Proof

1. What is the first proof?
*2. According to Annemarie's dad, what is good for the soul? What does he mean?
3. What does Miranda give the laughing man?
4. Why is Mom upset about Miranda talking to the laughing man?
5. Does Miranda think Mom should marry Richard?
6. Why does Miranda worry that Annemarie will not be there in the morning?
7. How does Annemarie think her father treats her? How does she think Miranda's mom treats Miranda?
8. Why does Jimmy lock Miranda and her friends out of his shop?
9. Whom does Jimmy accuse of stealing his bank?
10. Why does Annemarie get upset at Miranda?
11. Who is the kid wearing green suede boots? Who has a charge account at Gold's? Who has keys in her pocket?
12. What is the second proof?

## Things in an Elevator–Things That Heal

1. What does Miranda want to ask Annemarie?
2. Why is Mom upset at Miranda?
*3. Why do Miranda and Mom laugh about being late to meet Richard?
4. Who left the rose for Annemarie? Why?
5. How does Miranda help Alice Evans? Why does she do this?
6. What does Miranda write in her note to Julia?
7. Who stole Jimmy's bank?
8. What familiar item does Miranda see in Julia's room?
9. How does the laughing man save Sal?
10. Where does Miranda find the last note?
11. Why did the laughing man stand on the street corner every day?
12. Why did Sal avoid Miranda?

Name _____

*When You Reach Me*
Study Guide
page 4

## Things You Protect–Parting Gifts

1. What does Wheelie do that frightens Miranda? Why does Wheelie behave as she does?
*2. Do you think Marcus is responsible for the accident?
3. Why won't Mom allow the police to talk to Marcus?
4. Whom does Miranda try to forget? Why can't she forget?
5. What is the last proof?
6. Who accompanies Mom to *The $20,000 Pyramid*?
7. Who is "the magic thread" (p. 189)?
8. How much money does Mom win?
9. What is Miranda and Richard's secret plan?
10. What does Miranda find under the mailbox?
11. What do Miranda and Sal do when they pass the laughing man's mailbox?
*12. What will Miranda say when she hands Marcus the letter? What is the significance of this?

Name _____

*When You Reach Me*
Activity #10 • Critical Thinking
Use After Reading
*(Making Connections)*

## Effects of Reading

**Directions:** When reading, each part of a novel may affect you in a different way. Think about how parts of the novel affected you in different ways. Did some parts make you laugh? cry? want to do something to help someone? Below, list one part of the novel that touched each of the following parts of the body: your head (made you think), your heart (made you feel), your funny bone (made you laugh), or your feet (spurred you to action).

| Your head | Your heart |
|---|---|
| | |

| Your funny bone | Your feet |
|---|---|
| | |

Name _____

**When You Reach Me**
Activity #11 • Writing
Use After Reading
*(Write to Inform)*

## Newspaper

**Directions:** Write an article about Marcus discovering how to time travel. Answer the journalist's five questions: Who? What? Where? When? Why? Include details about Marcus' life from *When You Reach Me*.

## Future News

Wednesday, October 2 • Section A, Page 1

Name _____

***When You Reach Me***
Activity #12 • Literary Analysis
Use During and After Reading
*(Literary Devices)*

## Foreshadowing Chart

**Foreshadowing** is the literary technique of giving clues to coming events in a story.

**Directions:** What examples of foreshadowing do you recall from the story? If necessary, skim through the chapters to find examples of foreshadowing. List at least four examples below. Explain what clues are given, and then list the coming event that is suggested.

| Foreshadowing | Page # | Clues | Coming Event |
|---|---|---|---|
| | | | |
| | | | |
| | | | |
| | | | |
| | | | |
| | | | |
| | | | |
| | | | |

Name _____

***When You Reach Me***
Activity #13 • Character Analysis
Use During and After Reading
*(Character Analysis)*

## Character Analysis

**Directions:** Working in small groups, discuss the attributes of the characters listed below. In each character's box, write several words or phrases that describe him or her.

Name _____

*When You Reach Me*
Activity #14 • Character Analysis
Use After Reading
*(Character Analysis)*

## The Five Senses

**Directions:** On the lines below, describe what Miranda experiences through each of the five senses. Include examples for each sense as well as the page numbers on which they are found.

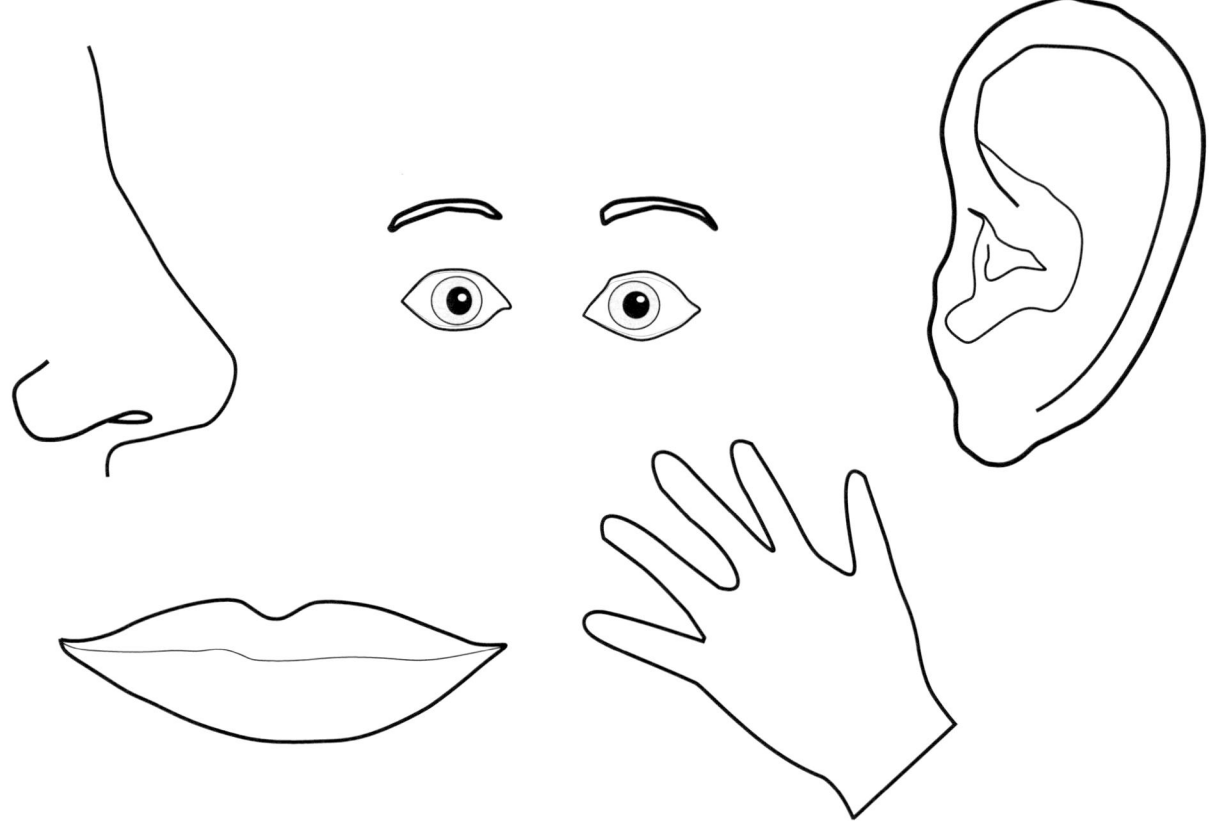

**Character:** Miranda

_____
_____
_____
_____
_____
_____

Name _____

**When You Reach Me**
Activity #15 • Comprehension
Use After Reading
*(Sequencing)*

## Sequencing Events

**Directions:** In the boxes below, illustrate main events throughout the story in the order they occurred in the novel. Write an explanation for each illustration on the corresponding line below the boxes.

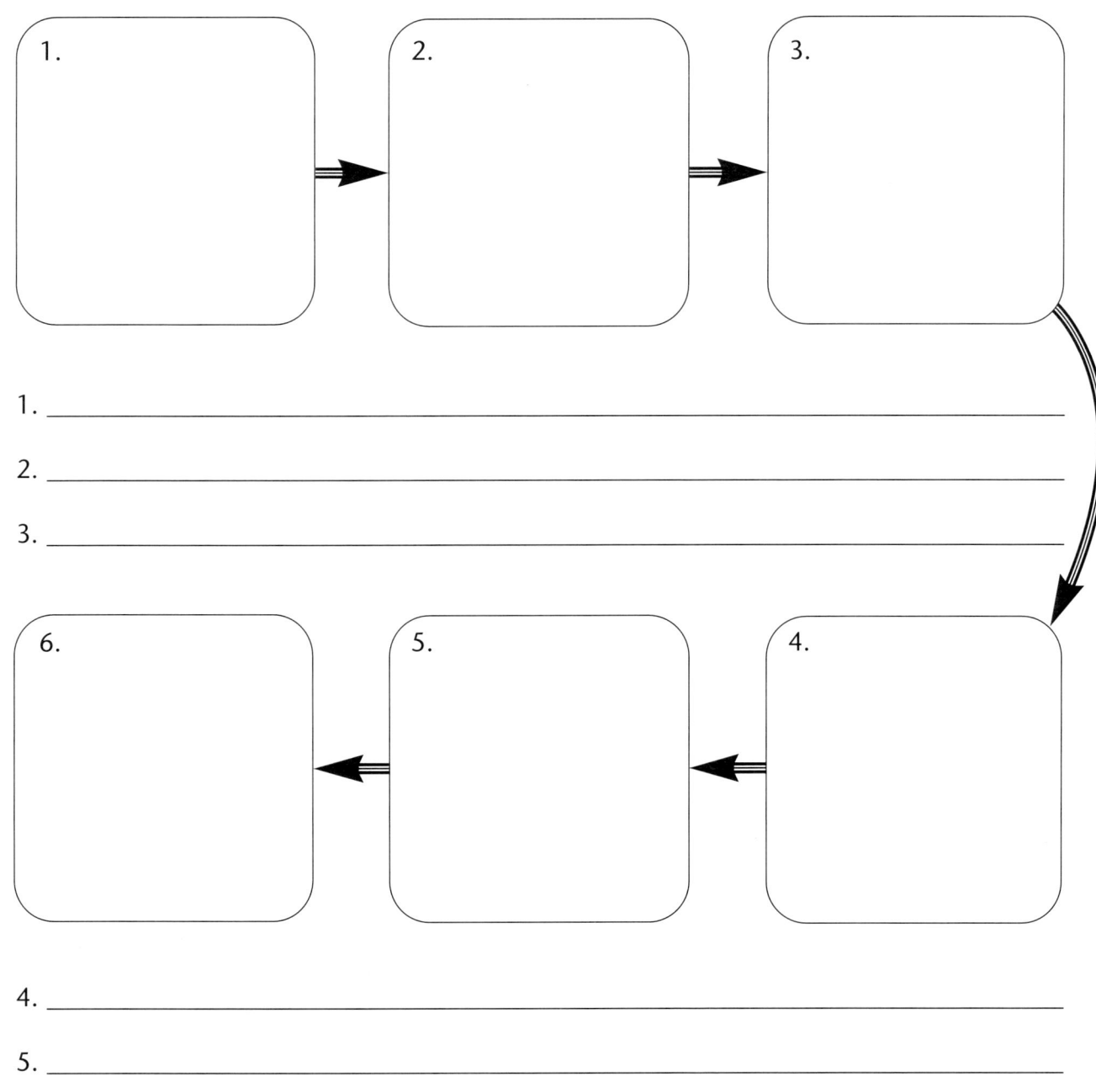

1. _____
2. _____
3. _____

4. _____
5. _____
6. _____

Name _____

**When You Reach Me**
Activity #16 • Character Analysis
Use After Reading
*(Character Analysis)*

## Character Growth

**Directions:** Characters often "grow" throughout a novel as they learn and change. In the tree rings below, write either examples of Miranda's growth or events that cause her growth. Write the examples or events in the order they occur in the novel.

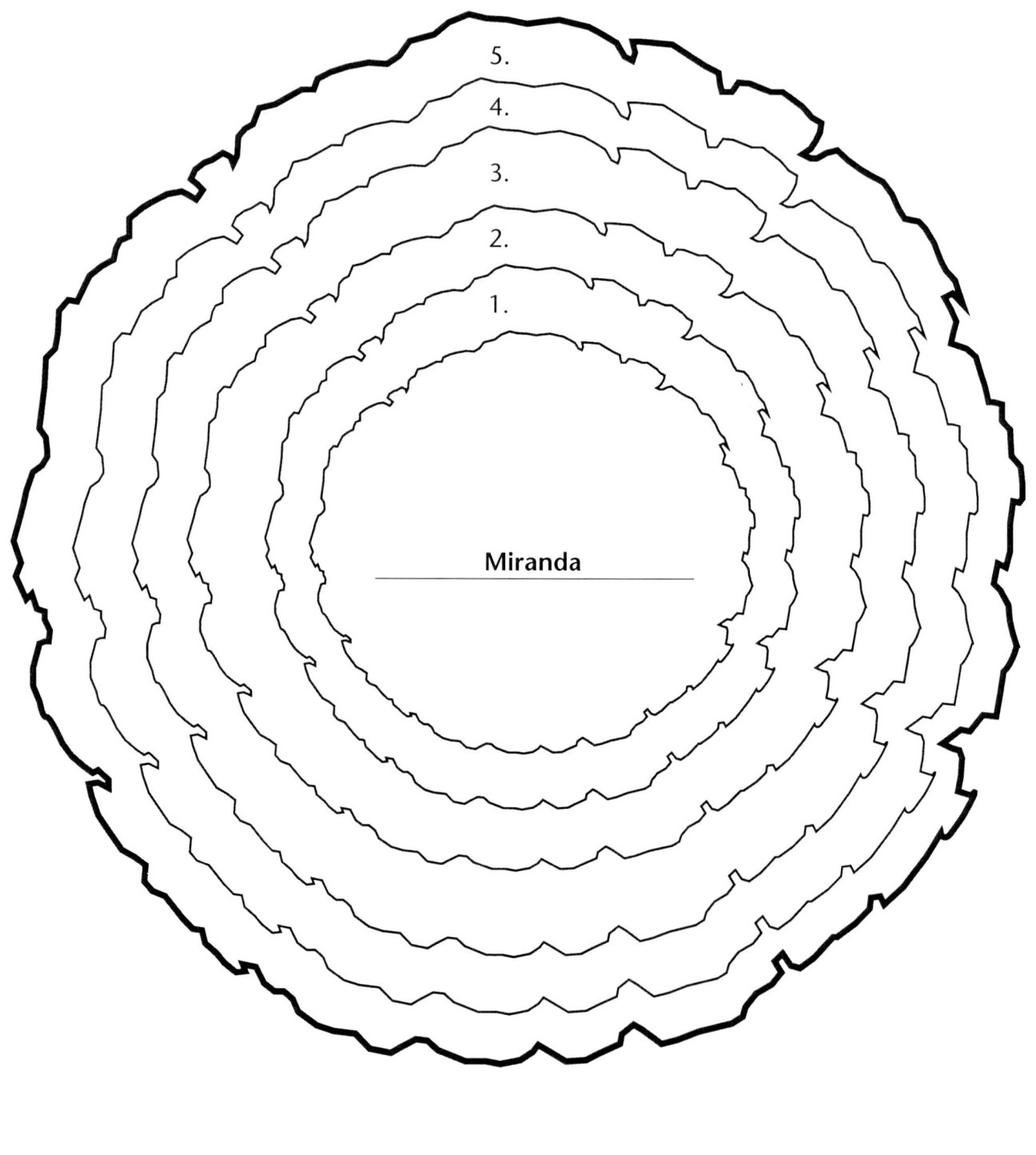

Name _____

**When You Reach Me**
Activity #17 • Critical Thinking
Use After Reading
*(Cause/Effect)*

## Rainstorming

**Directions:** Use the clouds below to track the effects of Marcus discovering how to time travel. Use the clouds on the left to show effects from Marcus' life as a child. Use the clouds on the right to show effects from Marcus' life as an adult.

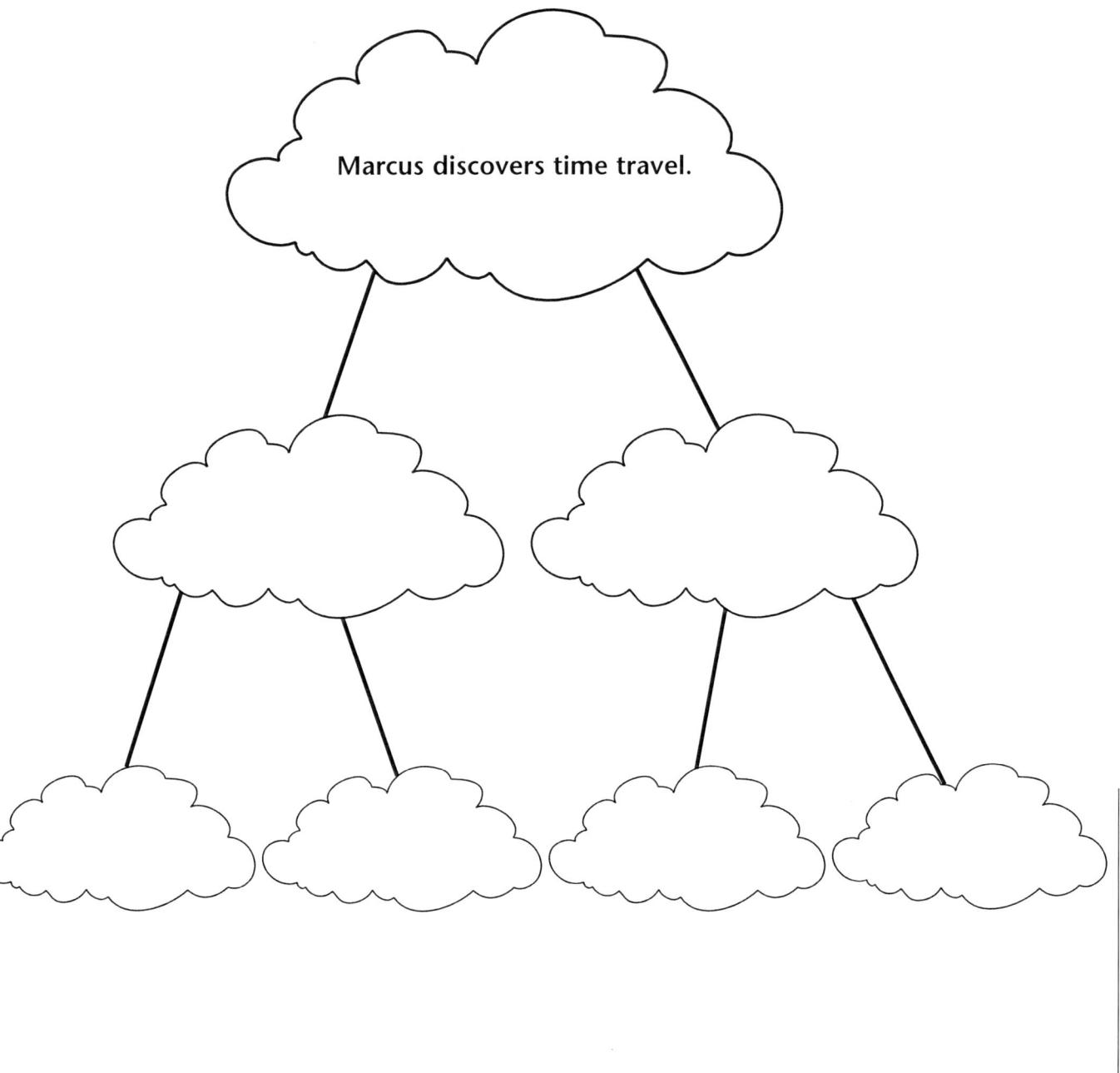

© Novel Units, Inc. 23

Name _____

**When You Reach Me**
Activity #18 • Literary Analysis
Use After Reading
*(Literary Elements)*

## Story Map

**Directions:** Complete the story map below.

**Characters**

- main _____
- main _____
- main _____
- minor _____
- minor _____
- minor _____

**Setting**

Date: _____
Place: _____
Other: _____

*When You Reach Me*

**Conflict(s)**

**Possible Themes**
(general statements the novel makes about life)

**Point of View**
_____

**Genre**
_____

**Author's Style and Tone**

Name _____

**When You Reach Me**
Activity #19 • Literary Analysis
Use After Reading
*(Literary Devices)*

## Literary Devices

**Directions:** Authors use literary devices to make their writing interesting and descriptive. Read the definitions of the literary devices listed below, and then find an example of each in the novel. Include the page number where you found the example.

| | |
|---|---|
| **Flashback:** The story switches to an event from the past, then returns to the present. *(Look for clues such as "She remembered the last time…" followed by a scene from the past.)* | |
| **Foreshadowing:** An event is hinted about before it happens. *(Example: His plan would work, unless his mother found out about it.)* | |
| **Rhetorical Question:** A question is asked for effect with no answer expected. *(Example: She looked at the jagged peak and asked, "Do you think I'm part mountain goat?")* | |
| **Metaphor:** A comparison is made between two unlike objects. *(Example: He was a human tree.)* | |
| **Simile:** A comparison is made between two unlike objects using the words "like" or "as." *(Example: The color of her eyes was like the cloudless sky.)* | |
| **Onomatopoeia:** Words sound like what they mean. *(Examples: buzz, hiss)* | |
| **Personification:** Human traits are given to an object. *(Example: The cloud cried.)* | |

© Novel Units, Inc.

Name _____

**When You Reach Me**
Activity #20 • Writing
Use After Reading
*(Write to Entertain)*

## It Was a Dark and Stormy Night

**Directions:** Miranda's favorite novel, *A Wrinkle in Time*, begins with "It was a dark and stormy night" (p. 8). This opening is a reference, or allusion, to the 1830 novel *Paul Clifford* by Edward Bulwer-Lytton that begins with the same line. Use the famous line to begin a story of your own.

Name _____

**When You Reach Me**
Quiz #1
Things You Keep in a Box–
Things That Make No Sense

*(Main Idea and Details)*
**A. True/False:** Mark each with a *T* for true or an *F* for false.

____ 1. April 27th: Studio TV-15 is Miranda's last proof.

____ 2. Miranda is named after the main character in her favorite novel.

____ 3. The laughing man has approximately 30 fillings in his teeth.

____ 4. Sal ends his friendship with Miranda on the day he gets punched.

____ 5. Annemarie asks Miranda to lunch because Julia is punishing her.

____ 6. Marcus tells Miranda that she is a smart kid.

____ 7. Jimmy pays Miranda and her friends with two-dollar bills.

____ 8. Miranda finds the first note before the apartment key is stolen.

____ 9. The second note states that Miranda cannot begin her letter yet.

____ 10. A robber stole Richard's work shoes from Miranda's apartment.

____ 11. Sal is afraid of Marcus.

____ 12. Julia has an epileptic seizure from eating too much bread.

____ 13. The third note lists three proofs.

____ 14. Julia uses her diamond necklace to explain time travel.

____ 15. The laughing man runs away from Marcus.

*(Character Analysis)*
**B. Open-Ended Comprehension:** Write your response on the lines below.
Explain what Miranda does to cope with losing Sal's friendship.

_____

_____

_____

_____

_____

_____

_____

Name _____

**When You Reach Me**
Quiz #2
The First Proof–Parting Gifts

*(Main Idea and Details)*
### A. Fill in the Blanks

1. The first proof is bread rolls in _____ backpack.

2. Miranda's mom is afraid of making _____.

3. Jimmy believes _____ stole his bank.

4. The second proof is "_____ _____" written in a copy of Miranda's favorite novel.

5. _____ leaves a rose for _____.

6. Miranda befriends _____ _____, a classmate whom she has ignored in the past.

7. Only _____ can defeat the evil IT in Miranda's novel.

8. _____ unintentionally chases _____ into the street.

9. A truck hits the _____ _____.

10. The four words scratched into the mailbox paint are _____, _____, _____, and _____.

11. Miranda finds the last note in _____ shoe.

12. In theory, _____ _____ is possible.

13. _____ is the laughing man.

14. Miranda's mom wins $10,000 on _____ _____ _____.

15. Being together because they want to be renews _____ and Miranda's friendship.

*(Drawing Conclusions)*
### B. Open-Ended Comprehension: Write your response on the lines below.

Explain why Miranda decides to write the letter.

_____

_____

_____

_____

Name _____

**When You Reach Me**
Novel Test

*(Character Analysis)*
**A. Matching:** Match each quotation to the correct character.

___ 1. "You can't accept the idea of arriving before you leave...."   a. Miranda

___ 2. "Polite is always worth something."   b. Sal

___ 3. "It *wasn't* normal. I didn't have any other friends!"   c. Annemarie

___ 4. "But being in jail can make them feel like a mistake is all they are."   d. Julia

___ 5. "You've been giving me dirty looks since like third grade!"   e. Colin

___ 6. "Try not to land in the broccoli."   f. Marcus

___ 7. "All the money in the world can't change a person's blood."   g. Miranda's mom

___ 8. "How about talking to the owner about giving us jobs?"   h. Richard

___ 9. "It's this crazy diet my dad read about, but it actually works."   i. Jimmy

___ 10. "Keys are power."   j. Belle

*(Summarize Major Ideas)*
**B. Identification:** Explain how each word or phrase listed below is important to the story. Write one or two sentences for each word or phrase.

11. friendship _____
_____

12. keys _____
_____

13. knots _____
_____

14. *The $20,000 Pyramid* _____
_____

15. time travel _____
_____

Name _____

***When You Reach Me***
Novel Test
page 2

**C. Multiple Choice:** Choose the BEST answer.

*(Main Idea and Details)*

____ 16. What does Miranda keep in a box under her bed?

    (a) her novel

    (b) mysterious notes

    (c) game show postcards

    (d) law school applications

*(Main Idea and Details)*

____ 17. Miranda's story begins on the day that

    (a) Sal got punched

    (b) Mom and Louisa met

    (c) the laughing man showed up

    (d) Mom hosted a tenant meeting

*(Main Idea and Details)*

____ 18. At the dentist's office, Marcus tells Miranda that

    (a) he wanted to hit Sal

    (b) she is a pretty smart kid

    (c) the girl in her novel lied

    (d) time travel is impossible

*(Cause/Effect)*

____ 19. Mom taking cookies and chips to the jail shows she is

    (a) caring

    (b) legal-minded

    (c) lonely

    (d) wealthy

Name _____

***When You Reach Me***
Novel Test
page 3

*(Cause/Effect)*
____ 20. Annemarie has an epileptic seizure because

    (a) Colin kissed Miranda

    (b) she ate too much bread

    (c) Julia and Miranda argue

    (d) she is stressed about schoolwork

*(Main Idea and Details)*
____ 21. Colin steals Jimmy's

    (a) tips

    (b) bread rolls

    (c) two-dollar bills

    (d) Fred Flintstone bank

*(Character Analysis)*
____ 22. Why does Miranda give the laughing man a sandwich?

    (a) He asks her for it.

    (b) Her mother tells her to.

    (c) She wants to do something good.

    (d) She feels guilty for being mean to Annemarie.

*(Main Idea and Details)*
____ 23. Whom does the laughing man save?

    (a) Julia

    (b) Marcus

    (c) Miranda

    (d) Sal

Name _____

**When You Reach Me**
Novel Test
page 4

*(Character Analysis)*

____ 24. Sal ended his friendship with Miranda because

    (a) Marcus punched him

    (b) Miranda has a new best friend

    (c) he wants more than one friend

    (d) bullies tease him about having a girlfriend

*(Character Analysis)*

____ 25. When Miranda's "veil" lifts, she realizes that

    (a) Dick Clark never ages

    (b) Marcus is the laughing man

    (c) Richard and Mom will get married

    (d) Mom won on *The $20,000 Pyramid*

Name _____

*When You Reach Me*
Novel Test
page 5

**D. Essay:** Write a well-developed essay for two of the following using a separate sheet of paper.

*(Cause/Effect)*
I. Think about events that happen in *When You Reach Me* and how one event causes others. Choose an event from the story. Write an essay explaining how this event causes others to happen. Use information from the novel to support your answer.

*(Theme)*
II. Write an essay about the theme of "second chances." Explain how characters and setting are used to develop this theme.

*(Setting)*
III. Write an essay about the importance of setting in *When You Reach Me*.

*(Character Analysis)*
IV. Miranda matures during the story. Write an essay that shows how Miranda grows up. Explain how changes in friendships contribute to her maturity.

*(Support Responses)*
V. Write an essay about the importance of Miranda's novel, *A Wrinkle in Time*, to the plot. Use examples from *When You Reach Me* to support your answer.

# Answer Key

**Activities #1–#2:** Answers will vary.

**Activity #3:** 1. a 2. b 3. a 4. a 5. c 6. c 7. c 8. c 9. b 10. c 11. b 12. b 13. b 14. c 15. a

**Activity #4:** Answers will vary.

**Activity #5:** 1. hate 2. harsh 3. a failure 4. a response 5. sidetracked 6. end 7. hazy 8. meanness 9. last longer 10. insulted 11. annoying

**Activity #6:** 1. precious 2. jailbird 3. triumphant 4. seizures 5. insane 6. teleportation 7. mimeographs 8. mystified 9. construct 10. circulation 11. justification 12. atoms 13. epilepsy

**Activity #7:** 1. dissolved 2. vision 3. racist 4. hypnotizing 5. valuable 6. dingy 7. sesame 8. appropriate 9. sincere 10. swaggered 11. miserable 12. remotely 13. microscopic 14. symbolize 15. hysterical; Synonyms: 2, 3, 4, 6, 7, 9, 12, 14, 15; Antonyms: 1, 5, 8, 10, 11, 13

**Activity #8:** Students will play the Vocabulary Concentration game.

**Activity #9:** Word maps will vary. Dictionary definitions: casually—seemingly indifferently; sprinted—dashed, raced; accusingly—reproachfully; anesthesia—drug that decreases sensitivity to pain; allegations—accusations, charges; embroidered—decorated by needlework; audience—viewers, spectators; podium—stand, platform; artificial—fake, simulated; autographs—signatures of famous persons; squawked—shrieked, protested; precise—exact; applications—formal requests; seam—joint, union

## Study Guide

**Things You Keep in a Box–Mom's Rules for Life in New York City:** 1. to be a contestant on *The $20,000 Pyramid* 2. notes; someone who is gone 3. Richard is handsome and intelligent; Richard taps his right knee as a reminder that his right leg is shorter than his left leg. 4. Mom hates her job; Answers will vary but should relate to whether stealing is ever right. 5. "It was a dark and stormy night" (p. 8). 6. when Miranda was born 7. inside the nozzle of the apartment's old fire hose 8. From the time they were babies, Miranda and Sal did everything together. 9. "Bookbag, pocketshoe, bookbag, pocketshoe" (p. 18). 10. tie and untie sailors' knots 11. the story Miranda is supposed to tell; Miranda and Sal's friendship 12. Miranda asks for the time.

**Things You Wish For–Things You Keep Secret:** 1. her straight, brown hair 2. Miranda and Richard have a secret plan for any money Mom wins on *The $20,000 Pyramid*. 3. The kid punched Sal. 4. Answers will vary. 5. Julia's family travels around the world, and Julia has fancy clothes and jewelry. 6. Miranda does not have Sal's company, and Julia punishes Annemarie by refusing to have lunch with her. 7. Answers will vary. Suggestions: Annemarie's friendship with Julia is important to her. Annemarie's parents have more money than Miranda's mom and buy Annemarie nice things. 8. $20,000 9. Main Street, a scale model of a city block 10. school secretary; the dentist's runner 11. Marcus acts as if he has never seen Miranda. 12. Miranda does a better job than most people discussing time travel with Marcus.

**Things That Smell–Messy Things:** 1. about giving jobs at the sandwich shop to him, Miranda, and Annemarie 2. After finding the door unlocked, Miranda is frightened and feels as if she is not alone in the apartment. 3. Mom discovers that the spare key hidden in the fire hose is missing. 4. sticking out of her library book 5. Miranda cannot make the V-cut that Jimmy uses on his sandwich rolls. 6. Angel 7. in Jimmy's bread delivery bag 8. two-dollar bills 9. The person sees the world as it really is. 10. "Swiss Miss" 11. Answers will vary but should include Miranda is interested in or likes Colin. 12. Answers will vary. Suggestions: Miranda is playing the girls' rotating friendship game. She is jealous of Julia and Annemarie's friendship.

**Invisible Things–Things That Make No Sense:** 1. Marcus is absorbed in a book as he walks to the dentist's office. 2. get out of his shop 3. Mom brings chips and cookies to pregnant women in jail and talks to them. 4. Richard's work shoes 5. because a naked man is once again running down Broadway 6. Annemarie briefly blacks out; Answers will vary, but students should infer that Julia told the school nurse. 7. Annemarie has epilepsy. 8. Colin; Answers will vary. 9. in her jacket pocket 10. "to travel, through space or time or both" (p. 99) 11. her diamond ring 12. Marcus wanted to see what would happen.

**The First Proof–The Second Proof:** 1. Miranda finds Jimmy's missing bread rolls in Colin's backpack. 2. pajamas; Answers will vary but should refer to pajamas being comforting and comfortable. 3. a sandwich 4. Mom does not want Miranda talking to strangers. She worries about Miranda's safety, especially since Miranda is on her own after school. 5. yes 6. Sal always went home during the night. 7. like a baby; like a real person 8. Jimmy believes one of them stole his bank. 9. Julia 10. Annemarie learns that Miranda's nickname for Julia is "Swiss Miss" and assumes the name has to do with Julia being black. 11. Julia; Annemarie; Miranda 12. "Tesser well" is written in a first edition of *A Wrinkle in Time* that Richard gives Miranda for Christmas.

**Things in an Elevator–Things That Heal:** 1. whether or not they are still friends 2. Miranda went to Annemarie's house without Mom's consent. 3. Answers will vary. Suggestion: Mom was angry that Miranda went out and lost track of time, then Mom forgets about meeting Richard. 4. Julia; Julia cares about Annemarie. 5. Miranda offers to go to the bathroom with Alice; Miranda realizes that ignoring Alice in the past was mean. 6. "truce" and Miranda's phone number 7. the laughing man 8. a beat up copy of *A Wrinkle in Time* just like Miranda's 9. The laughing man kicks Sal out of the oncoming truck's path. 10. in a shoe the laughing man stole from Miranda's apartment 11. to save Sal 12. Sal wants more than one friend.

**Things You Protect–Parting Gifts:** 1. Wheelie acts as if she does not know Marcus; Miranda realizes Wheelie is afraid for Marcus. 2. Answers will vary. Suggestion: Marcus did not intend for the accident to happen. However, the accident occurred because Marcus chased Sal. 3. Mom wants Marcus' parents present. 4. the laughing man; Miranda still needs to write the letter. 5. A postcard from *The $20,000 Pyramid* arrives with the date and studio number, April 27th: Studio TV-15, as predicted in Miranda's note. 6. Miranda, Richard, Louisa, and Sal 7. Marcus 8. $22,100 9. for Mom to use her game show winnings to return to law school 10. her missing apartment key and a picture of Julia as an old woman 11. Sal salutes; Miranda shakes her fist at the sky. 12. "Try not to land in the broccoli" (p. 197); Answers will vary but should refer to Miranda and Marcus' first conversation about *A Wrinkle in Time* and time travel.

**Note:** Responses to Activities #10–#20 will vary. Suggested responses are given when applicable.

**Activities #10–#11:** Answers will vary.

**Activity #12:** Examples: 1. The laughing man's crazy laugh reveals "about thirty fillings in his teeth"; page 16; Marcus makes repeated trips to the school dentist; Marcus is the laughing man. 2. The laughing man always mumbles "bookbag, pocketshoe"; page 18; Miranda finds notes in a library book, Jimmy's bread bag, and her coat pocket; Miranda realizes the last note is in Richard's stolen shoe. 3. Students are kept on campus because of a naked man running down Broadway; page 35; Miranda sees a naked man briefly appear and disappear next to the laughing man; Time travel is a difficult trip that affects a person's mind and nothing, including clothes, can be brought along. 4. Marcus stares at Julia as she explains time travel to Miranda; page 103; The laughing man tells Miranda that he is old and not to worry because "she" is gone; Marcus and Julia are together in the future.

**Activity #13:** Examples: Miranda—latchkey child, intelligent, observant; Mom—loving, moody, civic-minded; Richard—caring, joker, knowledgeable; Sal—timid, subtle, athletic; Annemarie—sweet, epileptic, artistic; Julia—wealthy, faithful friend, brash; Marcus—brainy, deep thinker, loner; Jimmy—creepy, racist, selfish

**Activity #14:** Examples: Smell—Miranda loves the "food-but-not-food" smell of dry-cleaner exhaust; Sight—Seeing Julia look at Annemarie makes Miranda want to befriend Alice Evans; Sound—The bouncing of Sal's basketball comforts Miranda as their last connection; Taste—Mustard sauce burning Miranda's lips is worth being at Annemarie's house; Touch—The stiffness of the notes feels as if the papers had once been wet.

**Activity #15:** Examples: 1. Marcus punches Sal. 2. Miranda finds a note in her library book. 3. Julia uses her diamond ring to explain time travel. 4. The laughing man saves Sal. 5. Miranda's mom wins $22,100. 6. Miranda writes a letter to Marcus.

**Activity #16:** Examples: 1. Losing Sal's friendship forces Miranda to leave her comfort zone and make friends with Annemarie. 2. Marcus says time travel is possible, and Miranda begins thinking about the world in new ways. 3. Jimmy's accusation that Julia is a thief because she is black shows Miranda the harm in judging people. 4. At the school assembly, Miranda realizes that ignoring Alice Evans is the same as being mean to her. 5. Miranda shows compassion for Marcus, whom she considers a hero with an unhappy ending.

**Activity #17:** Examples: Middle Left Cloud—Marcus analyzes *A Wrinkle in Time*, studies physics, and determines time travel is possible; First Lower Cloud—Marcus will read and understand Miranda's letter; Second Lower Cloud—Marcus witnesses the laughing man's death; Middle Right Cloud—Marcus travels back in time but has difficulties, such as arriving naked and with an unsound mind; Third Lower Cloud—The laughing man flees from Marcus; Fourth Lower Cloud—The laughing man saves Sal.

**Activity #18:** Some answers may vary. Characters: Miranda, Marcus, the laughing man, Sal, Annemarie, Julia; Setting: 1970s. New York City; Conflicts: Miranda receives ominous notes, one of which asks her to write a letter; Mom needs to win *The $20,000 Pyramid*; Miranda loses her best friend Sal and becomes tangled in other friendships; Miranda deals with homelessness, bullies, racism, and death; Miranda struggles to understand the complexities of time travel; Possible Themes: time travel, friendship, family, city life, second chances, coming of age; Point of View: first person and second person; Author's Style and Tone: narrative using present and past tense, conversational, thought-provoking, ominous, humorous; Genre: mystery with elements of realistic, historical, and science fiction

**Activity #19:** Examples: Flashback—"Mom cried the first time she saw our apartment" (p. 14); Foreshadowing— "Like you're supposed to be eating sandwiches and drinking soda" (p. 77); Rhetorical Question—"You counting those rolls or memorizing them?" (p. 68); Metaphor— "Keys are power." (p. 4); Simile—"...the apartment felt like a warm hug…" (p. 152); Onomatopoeia—"[Mom] clomps down the hall—she's on a clog kick lately..." (p. 5); Personification—"My brain has a way of talking to me like that" (p. 31).

**Activity #20:** Stories will vary.

**Quiz #1: A.** 1. T 2. F 3. T 4. T 5. F 6. T 7. F 8. F 9. T 10. T 11. T 12. F 13. T 14. F 15. T **B.** Answers will vary. Examples: Miranda prepares Mom for *The $20,000 Pyramid*. She helps Belle at the market, makes friends with Annemarie and Colin, and works at the sandwich shop.

**Quiz #2: A.** 1. Colin's 2. mistakes 3. Julia 4. Tesser well 5. Julia; Annemarie 6. Alice Evans 7. love 8. Marcus; Sal 9. laughing man 10. Book, Bag, Pocket, Shoe 11. Richard's 12. time travel 13. Marcus 14. *The $20,000 Pyramid* 15. Sal **B.** Answers will vary. Examples: Miranda hopes writing the letter will help her forget the laughing man. When she solves the mystery, she understands that the laughing man will know everything in advance because of her letter. Though the laughing man is gone, Miranda can still give the letter to Marcus.

**Novel Test: A.** 1. f (p. 105) 2. j (p. 151) 3. b (p. 169) 4. g (p. 85) 5. d (p. 93) 6. a (p. 197) 7. i (p. 129) 8. e (p. 54) 9. c (p. 95) 10. h (p. 4) **B.** Answers will vary. Examples: 11. friendship—Changing friendships broaden Miranda's experiences and help her to mature. In the end, she and Sal have a better, healthier friendship. 12. keys—Richard says, "Keys are power" (p. 4) representing acceptance into Miranda's family. Miranda is a latchkey child, and the need to hide a spare key, which is stolen, adds suspense to the story. 13. knots—Richard teaching Miranda to tie sailors' knots demonstrates their good relationship. Miranda picks up Richard's habit of tying and untying knots while working out problems. The knots may also symbolize the mystery Miranda must unravel. 14. *The $20,000 Pyramid*—The game show provides Mom with a way to better her financial circumstances. That Dick Clark never ages lifts Miranda's "veil," allowing her to solve the mystery. The game show establishes the 1970s setting and provides interesting chapter titles that tie the story together. 15. time travel—*A Wrinkle in Time*, with its time-travel theme, is the basis of Miranda's initial conversations with Marcus. Without time travel, Sal would have died. The complexities of time travel teach Miranda new ways of thinking and introduce her to physics. **C.** 16. b 17. a 18. b 19. a 20. b 21. b 22. c 23. d 24. c 25. b **D.** Essays will vary. Refer to the scoring rubric on page 38 of this guide.

# Linking Novel Units® Student Packets to National and State Reading Assessments

During the past several years, an increasing number of students have faced some form of state-mandated competency testing in reading. Many states now administer state-developed assessments to measure the skills and knowledge emphasized in their particular reading curriculum. This Novel Units® guide includes open-ended comprehension questions that correlate with state-mandated reading assessments. The rubric below provides important information for evaluating responses to open-ended comprehension questions. Teachers may also use scoring rubrics provided for their own state's competency test.

## Scoring Rubric for Open-Ended Items

| | |
|---|---|
| **3-Exemplary** | Thorough, complete ideas/information<br>Clear organization throughout<br>Logical reasoning/conclusions<br>Thorough understanding of reading task<br>Accurate, complete response |
| **2-Sufficient** | Many relevant ideas/pieces of information<br>Clear organization throughout most of response<br>Minor problems in logical reasoning/conclusions<br>General understanding of reading task<br>Generally accurate and complete response |
| **1-Partially Sufficient** | Minimally relevant ideas/information<br>Obvious gaps in organization<br>Obvious problems in logical reasoning/conclusions<br>Minimal understanding of reading task<br>Inaccuracies/incomplete response |
| **0-Insufficient** | Irrelevant ideas/information<br>No coherent organization<br>Major problems in logical reasoning/conclusions<br>Little or no understanding of reading task<br>Generally inaccurate/incomplete response |

# Notes

# Notes